We Can Cook!

by Abbie Rushton

illustrated by Emily Cooksey

Aiden has a cookbook.

Quick Fish Dish

You will need ...

fish

leeks

carrots

Can we cook thick chips as well?
Yes!

1. Cook the chips.

Dad peels.

He chops the chips into chunks.

Aiden coats the thick chips.

He puts them in the tin.

The chips go in to cook.

2. Cook the fish.

Aiden dips the fish in egg.

We need to coat the fish.
Look at my foot! It is a mess!

Aiden coats the fish.

Dad cooks the fish in a pan.

3. Cook the leeks and carrots.

Dad chops the leeks and carrots.

Aiden puts them in a pan.
The leeks and carrots cook.

Dad gets the chip tin.
He puts it on a wooden mat.

This looks good!
Tuck in, Dad!

Cook the chips

1. ....
2. chop
3. coat

Cook the fish

1. dip
2. ....

Cook the leeks and carrots

1. peel
2. ....

chop   coat   peel

Encourage students to choose the correct word to complete each step of the recipe.